Communicate!
World Leaders Speak

Nicole Sipe

Publishing Credits

Rachelle Cracchiolo, M.S.Ed., *Publisher*
Conni Medina, M.A.Ed., *Managing Editor*
Nika Fabienke, Ed.D., *Series Developer*
June Kikuchi, *Content Director*
Susan Daddis, M.A.Ed., *Editor*
Kevin Pham, *Graphic Designer*

TIME is a registered trademark of TIME Inc. Used under license.

Image Credits: Front cover, Action Sports Photography/Shutterstock; p.1 Arindam Banerjee/Shutterstock; pp.4–5 Paul Schutzer/Time Life Pictures/Getty Images; pp.6–7 MediaPunch Inc/Alamy; pp.8–9 Paul Schutzer/The LIFE Picture Collection/Getty Images; pp.10–11 Interfoto/Alamy; p.14 (insert) Courtesy Time Inc.; p.15 Nicole Craine/WireImage; p.18 Chronicle/Alamy; p.20 (bottom) Manchester Daily Express/SSPL/Getty Images; p.21 Bettmann/Getty Images; p.22 (bottom) Andrea Raffin/Shutterstock; p.23 Rob Kim/Getty Images; pp.24–25 US Army Photo/Alamy; pp.26–27 courtesy Signal Corps Collections, USMA Archives; p.28 PA Images/Alamy; p.33 North Wind Picture Archives; pp.34–35 Cathy Murphy/Getty Images; pp.36–37 Tony Avelar/Bloomberg via Getty Images; pp.38–39 Jamie Schwaberow/NCAA Photos via Getty Images; p.41 Otto Herschan/Getty Images; all other images from iStock and/or Shutterstock.

All companies and products mentioned in this book are registered trademarks of their respective owners or developers and are used in this book strictly for editorial purposes; no commercial claim to their use is made by the author or the publisher.

Library of Congress Cataloging-in-Publication Data

Names: Sipe, Nicole, author. | Sipe, Nicole, editor.
Title: Communicate! : world leaders speak / Nicole Sipe [editor of compilation].
Other titles: World leaders speak
Description: Huntington Beach, CA : Teacher Created Materials, [2019] | Includes bibliographical references and index. | Audience: 4 to 6.
Identifiers: LCCN 2017056311 (print) | LCCN 2018028894 (ebook) | ISBN 9781425849986 (e-book) | ISBN 9781425849986 (pbk.)
Subjects: LCSH: Speeches, addresses, etc.--Juvenile literature. | Speeches. sears
Classification: LCC PN6122 (ebook) | LCC PN6122 .S584 2019 (print) | DDC 808.85--dc23
LC record available at https://lccn.loc.gov/2017056311

Teacher Created Materials

5301 Oceanus Drive
Huntington Beach, CA 92649-1030
www.tcmpub.com

ISBN 978-1-4258-4998-6

© 2019 Teacher Created Materials, Inc.

Table of Contents

Lend Me Your Ears! 4

From the White House 6

Speeches Abroad 18

A Call to Arms 24

Agents of Change 30

The Power of Words 40

Glossary 42

Index 44

Check It Out! 46

Try It! 47

About the Author 48

Lend Me Your Ears!

Here's a riddle for you: *What is something that can make you laugh, cry, feel angry, feel inspired, and make you think—all at the same time?* If you said, "a speech," then you're right! A speech can make you feel a multitude of emotions. A speech can **motivate** you to action, persuade you to consider old ideas in new ways, and inspire you to change the world. In other words, speeches are very powerful!

History is full of leaders from around the world who have given inspiring speeches. These prominent men and women used the power of the spoken word to impact others. Although almost anyone can speak, it takes a substantial amount of skill to be a great orator.

Orators take ordinary words and weave them into brilliant speeches. Their speeches tell stories, relay information, and **influence** people's lives.

Communication Long Ago

In ancient Greek and Roman times, the best way to relay information was by delivering speeches in person. Giving a speech was considered a very important skill. It was a subject that was taught in schools.

Dr. Martin Luther King Jr. gives a speech in Washington, DC in 1957.

From the White House

Some of the most memorable speeches have come from U.S. presidents and first ladies. These leaders are always in the spotlight. They have many chances to speak out about any issue. And when the White House speaks, people listen!

John F. Kennedy

It was a cold and clear day in Washington, DC, on January 20, 1961. A crowd was gathered outside the Capitol. Everyone was waiting to hear the new president speak. Television cameras were rolling, ready to capture a moment in history. John F. Kennedy stepped up to the **podium**. It was his first official day as president of the United States.

Cold and Bold

Eight inches of snow fell the night before Kennedy's speech. Despite the frosty weather, Kennedy delivered his speech outdoors. He chose not to wear a jacket or hat while at the podium.

John F. Kennedy

THINK LINK

> Have you ever heard a speech that inspired you? Why were you inspired?

> Why is it important for world leaders to make speeches?

> How can a powerful speech influence the way people think?

Kennedy and his wife, Jacqueline, walk to his inauguration.

Kennedy's **inauguration** speech addressed the big issue that was on everyone's mind at the time: the Cold War. The Cold War was a time of tension and competition between the United States and the Soviet Union.

During his speech, Kennedy said that he would be a leader of peace. He challenged the world to unite and cooperate instead of divide. This was a **turbulent** time in history when Americans were weary and looking for solutions. However, Kennedy could not offer a quick fix to the nation's problems. Instead, he offered his people hope—but he needed their help.

Then, Kennedy spoke these memorable words: "And so, my fellow Americans: ask not what your country can do for you. Ask what you can do for your country."

It was a call to duty. The president was challenging the people in his country. To create a better world, citizens must contribute and make things happen for the better.

Only a Lad

Kennedy was 43 years old when he became president. He is the youngest elected president in U.S. history! The average age of a president on the first day on the job is 55 years old.

Ronald Reagan

In June 1987, Ronald Reagan gave one of his most famous speeches. He challenged Soviet Union leader Mikhail Gorbachev by saying, "Mr. Gorbachev, tear down this wall!" The concrete wall in Germany was built in 1961 to keep East Berlin and West Berlin separate. At the time, the Soviet Union backed East Germany, and the United States backed West Germany. The wall was about 15 feet (5 meters) high and covered in barbed wire. It went 28 miles (45 kilometers) through the city of Berlin.

Reagan's challenge came during a visit to Berlin. He was asked to speak at a **ceremony** honoring the 750th anniversary of the city. Reagan gave his speech on the West side of the wall. His words were heard by people on both sides through speakers.

In 1989, East and West Germans tore down the Berlin Wall. It was the start of an era of peace in Berlin.

A Tale of Two Cities

The West side of the Berlin Wall was covered in art and graffiti. The East side, however, was blank. This is because people on the West side could easily access the wall, but people on the East side were not allowed to touch or even go near the wall.

Reagan waves to a crowd at the Berlin Wall.

Protect the President

Reagan stood in front of two bulletproof panes of glass when he gave his speech in Berlin. The glass was meant to shield the president from snipers who might target him from the east side of the Berlin Wall.

Abraham Lincoln

On March 4, 1865, Abraham Lincoln took to the podium after being elected to a second term as president. Four years earlier, he had given a very different speech as the country was on the brink of the Civil War; now, that war was coming to an end. People wanted to know how the nation would move forward.

Lincoln started by stating the cause for war: "One eighth of the whole population were colored slaves…. All knew that this interest was, somehow, the cause of the war." He then said that the North and the South must work together to make sure formerly enslaved people have a place in society.

The most famous lines from his speech came at the end: "With malice toward none; with charity for all…to do all which may achieve and cherish a just, and a lasting peace, among ourselves, and with all nations." He urged all Americans to do what was morally right.

Lincoln tried to balance his words. He did not blame the South for the Civil War, nor did he praise the pending victory by the North. In one of the shortest inauguration speeches ever, this president did his best to move the country forward together.

Gettysburg Address

Lincoln wrote the Gettysburg Address to honor Union soldiers who died in the battle at Gettysburg. It is his most famous speech as well as his shortest. It was just 272 words long and took only two minutes to deliver.

A Face in the Crowd

John Wilkes Booth sat in a balcony above President Lincoln during the second inaugural address. Booth wanted the United States to stay the way it was before the Civil War. At the time of this speech, Booth was involved in a plot to kidnap President Lincoln. Instead, Lincoln's speech angered Booth so much that one month later, Booth would shoot and kill the president.

John Wilkes Booth

Abraham Lincoln

Barack Obama

On March 7, 2015, thousands of people were gathered at the Edmund Pettus Bridge in Selma, Alabama. They were there to hear President Barack Obama speak.

The bridge had been the site of civil rights marches 50 years earlier. It was also the site of what would be known as "Bloody Sunday." This was a day when six hundred peaceful marchers were attacked by police officers as they marched for voting rights.

Obama spoke to **commemorate** the event. "Fifty years from Bloody Sunday, our march is not yet finished. …But we are getting closer," he said. "Our job is easier because somebody already got us through that first mile. Somebody already got us over that bridge."

The civil rights marches in Selma led to the passage of the Voting Rights Act of 1965. The law helped to protect voting rights for everyone, especially African Americans in the South.

Senator Obama

Before Obama became president, he was an Illinois state senator for eight years. After that, he became a U.S. senator. As a state senator, he was known for being able to work with people from both political parties. He worked to help children, the elderly, and unions. Obama continued this work as a U.S. senator and later as president.

By the Numbers

Obama served two terms as president. During his first year as president, he gave 411 speeches, talks, and remarks. By the time he left the White House, he had given 1,852 speeches, talks, and remarks.

Obama giving his speech in Selma.

You Don't Say!

Delivering a memorable speech involves more than just speaking words. In fact, how you say something is oftentimes more important than *what* you say. Communication can be divided into three parts: words, tone of voice, and body language.

Your voice and body language matter when speaking to the public. Great orators know this, so they use their bodies in specific ways when they are addressing the public.

Gesture occasionally to get a point across.

Important parts of the speech are memorized.

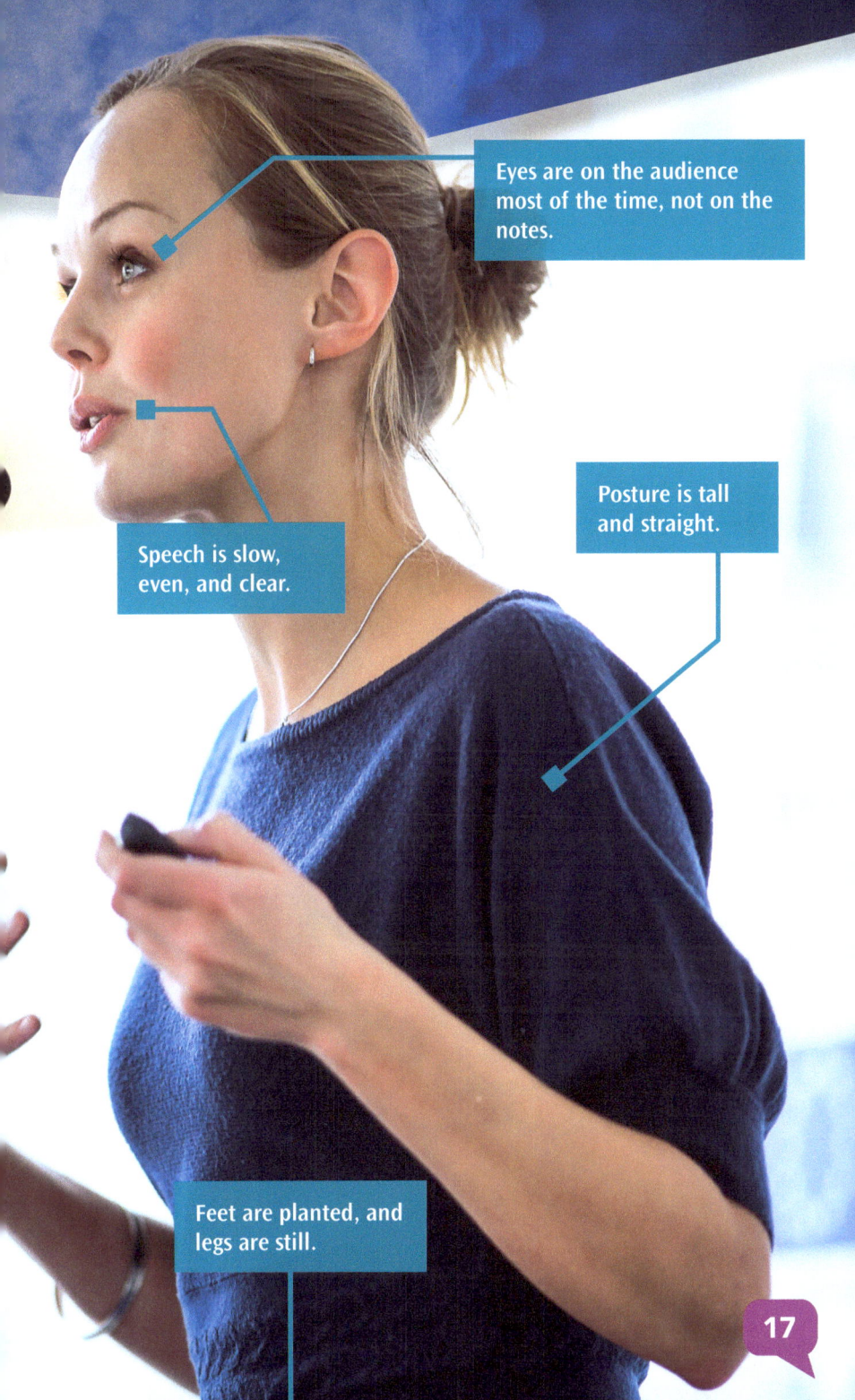

Speeches Abroad

In countries around the world, there are leaders with information and ideas to share. Speeches by these world leaders have the power to start wars, spark peace, and change history.

Margaret Thatcher

What if you gave a speech that was so good it earned you a nickname? This is what happened to Margaret Thatcher after she delivered her speech "Britain Awake."

After her 1976 speech at a town hall meeting in London, Thatcher became known as the Iron Lady. Thatcher spoke about the danger of the Soviet Union to the world. At the time, Great Britain was in the middle of the Cold War. This was a time when Western countries, such as Britain, did not get along with **communist** countries, such as the Soviet Union.

In 1976, Thatcher gave a speech to a women's organization.

Thatcher was well-known to go on little sleep—only about four hours a night! The average person needs about seven to nine hours of sleep. Getting enough sleep boosts a person's physical and mental health. Look at the clocks to answer the questions.

- Why do you think these people get less sleep than average?
- What pattern(s), if any, do you notice?
- Would these leaders be more effective if they got more sleep? Explain your reasoning.
- How do you think kids function on just 4 to 5 hours of sleep?

Thatcher's speech came at a time when the Soviet Union and Western countries had made a **pact** to be more peaceful with each other. Many people thought this meant that the Cold War would end soon. Thatcher did not believe that the Soviet Union really wanted peace with the Western world. She advised Britain to continue to be on guard.

"The Russians are bent on world dominance," she said in her speech. "They are rapidly acquiring the means to become the most powerful **imperial** nation the world has seen."

Thatcher's daring speech would help her secure a place as prime minister (PM) of Britain in 1979. She was elected for three terms and continued her role as PM for 11 years. She was the longest-serving PM in Britain's history and the first woman in Britain to serve in that role.

You're Never Too Young

Thatcher's interest in politics began at a young age. When she was 10 years old, she helped with a political **campaign**. Her father, who was a mayor at one time, was one of her inspirations for becoming a politician.

Thatcher (left) and her sister Muriel

Thatcher speaks at a conference.

Justin Trudeau

Equal rights for men and women is an important issue to Justin Trudeau. He became prime minister of Canada in 2015. He is a big supporter of gender equality.

One of Trudeau's best speeches was about this issue. He spoke at the HeForShe event in September 2016. HeForShe is a campaign that was started by UN Women, a part of the United Nations. The goal is to encourage men to help women succeed. The idea is that when women succeed, everyone benefits.

"We know if kids grow up in a more equal world, it is a better world," Trudeau said in his speech.

He asked for help in making the world a more equal place. "I think that everybody should be in the business of improving opportunities for women and girls," he said. "When women and girls get ahead, everyone does better in society. It's not just about women's issues. It's about all of our issues."

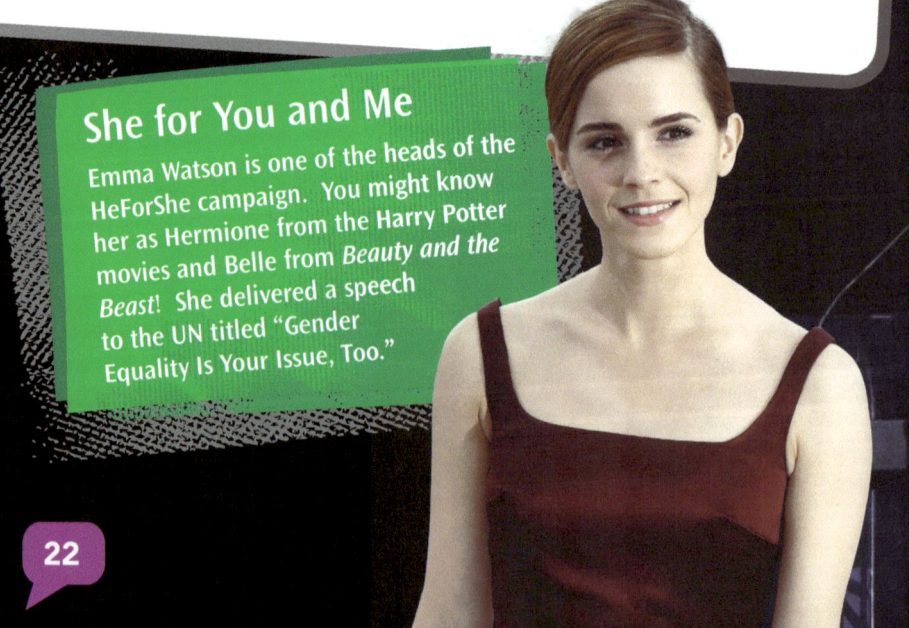

She for You and Me

Emma Watson is one of the heads of the HeForShe campaign. You might know her as Hermione from the Harry Potter movies and Belle from *Beauty and the Beast*! She delivered a speech to the UN titled "Gender Equality Is Your Issue, Too."

Welcome to the Future

Trudeau made news when he hired an equal number of men and women to serve in his office. No Canadian politician had ever done that before! When asked why gender equality was so important to him, he said, "Because it's 2015."

Trudeau delivers his speech on gender equality.

A Call to Arms

Sometimes, speeches are used to inspire people. Wartime is one of those times. Military leaders have used the power of words to motivate their troops during times of war—as well as times of peace.

Douglas MacArthur

It was so quiet, you could have heard a pin drop during Douglas MacArthur's speech at the U.S. Military Academy at West Point in New York. Everyone was focused on MacArthur as the army general spoke to the 2,100 cadets in May 1962. MacArthur had made the military his life. On this day, he was being awarded one of West Point's top awards. This speech was to be his last address to West Point.

West Point was a special place to MacArthur. He graduated from there in 1903 and served as its **superintendent** for three years. This was his big farewell.

General of the Army

MacArthur was a five-star general, which is the highest rank in the army. Only four other people have achieved this rank in U.S. history.

General MacArthur speaks to a large crowd in Chicago.

Stamp of Approval

You know you've made it big when your face appears on a stamp! MacArthur is on the six-cent U.S. stamp, which was issued in 1971. He also appears on stamps from Korea and the Philippines.

Copy That, Mom

In 1899, MacArthur moved from Texas to New York to attend West Point. Not wanting to be left behind, his mom packed her bags and moved right along with him! She lived in a hotel situated near West Point during the four years when MacArthur was a student.

General MacArthur inspects the cadet parade formation before his speech.

The 82-year-old retired general spoke for 34 minutes without looking at his notes. He spoke from his experience. He spoke from his heart.

"Duty, honor, country." These three words were very important to MacArthur's speech, so much so that he repeated them seven different times! "Duty, honor, country" is also important to West Point, as it is the school's motto.

MacArthur told the cadets to keep "duty, honor, country" in their hearts and minds. These three words would build their character and shape them into **noble** protectors of the nation. "They make you strong enough to know when you are weak, and brave enough to face yourself when you are afraid," MacArthur said.

MacArthur's "Duty, Honor, Country" speech was one of the most memorable speeches of his military career.

Like Father, Like Son

MacArthur received the Medal of Honor. His father, also a general in the army, received the award, too. They are one of two father-son duos to receive this honor. This award goes to leaders who act in courageous and heroic ways.

Collins stands at the Iraqi border two days after the war started.

Quick Thinking
Collins delivered his speech without planning or notes. It was not recorded, either. Collins's speech might have been lost forever if a journalist who was with the troops had not scribbled it down as the colonel was speaking!

Tim Collins

It was March 19, 2003, the day before the start of the second Iraq War. Tim Collins, a British Army colonel, stood before his troops to speak. His men formed a U-shaped huddle around him.

Collins knew the following day would be difficult because war is brutal. He wanted his troops fired up to fight, but he also wanted them to remember that they would be fighting against other humans. Collins told his troops: "The enemy should be in no doubt that we are his **nemesis** and that we are bringing about his rightful destruction."

But war does not mean losing your **humanity** and **empathy**. Collins continued his message: "We are going to Iraq to liberate and not to conquer....Show respect for them," he said.

Collins's address to his troops is considered one of the most inspiring speeches of the Iraq War. His speech was so admired that it once hung in the Oval Office of the White House.

Made for TV

Collins is a TV star...well, sort of. British actor Kenneth Branagh played Collins in a TV movie series called *10 Days to War*. The series, which aired in Britain, focused on real events that happened during the Iraq War.

Agents of Change

What is an agent of change? It is a person who asks questions, speaks up, and makes a positive difference in the world. Some of these "movers and shakers" hold high-ranking positions, and some don't. Some are more well-known than others, but all are leaders in their own right.

Frederick Douglass

On July 5, 1852, six hundred people gathered to hear Frederick Douglass speak. They had paid $12\frac{1}{2}$ cents each to hear the anti-slavery leader and author talk about a **compelling** topic: what the Fourth of July meant to black people in America.

Standing at the podium, Douglass started by praising the Founding Fathers. But then, the fiery orator got to the real reason behind why he chose to speak that day.

"This Fourth [of] July is yours, not mine. You may rejoice, I must mourn.…Do you mean, citizens, to mock me, by asking me to speak today?"

Little Reader

Douglass learned how to read as a child, which was illegal for an enslaved person. He carried a dictionary in his back pocket wherever he went. He would practice writing on boards, fences, and the ground.

Escape!

In September 1838, Douglass began his escape from slavery. In Baltimore, he dressed as a free black sailor and made sure to carry papers to prove he was free. His trip put him on a train and a ferry. Along the way, he saw two men he worked for, which made him nervous. He was sure that one recognized him, "but had not heart to betray me." Douglass arrived in New York in less than 24 hours. He eventually bought his freedom.

Douglass told the crowd that black people could not really celebrate a day meant for freedom. The Fourth of July for a black person was, "a day that reveals to him, more than all other days in the year, the gross **injustice** and cruelty to which he is the constant victim."

At the time, slavery was still legal in the United States. Most slaveholders did not allow their slaves to join in celebrations. Even in Northern states where blacks were free, many of them were not welcome to join in if white people were there.

Douglass, a former slave, was an abolitionist. This was a person who wanted slavery to end right away. He wanted all slaves to be free. In the 1850s, this idea was considered **radical**. During his speech, Douglass spoke to a mostly white audience about the wrongness of slavery. He wanted them to support the idea of abolishing it.

Slavery ended in 1865, more than a decade after Douglass's speech. His words live on in history and resonate today.

Happy Birthday
Like many people who were born into slavery, Douglass did not know his actual birthday. So he chose a day for himself! He picked February 14.

Douglass speaks to a group in England about his life as a slave.

Professional Speaker

After slavery ended, Douglass made his living giving speeches. He usually spent half the year traveling and speaking at events. He would make anywhere from $50 to $100 per speech.

Cesar Chavez

Cesar Chavez gave much of his life to improving the lives of **migrant** farm workers. He is known for starting a union for farm workers. A union is a group of workers who come together. As a group, they ask for better pay and safer working conditions from their employers.

In November 1984, Chavez spoke to the Commonwealth Club of California. During his speech, he described the terrible working conditions of migrant farm workers. He said, "Vicious rats gnaw at them as they sleep. They walk miles to buy food at inflated prices. And they carry in water from irrigation pumps. Child labor is still common in many farm areas."

Chavez's goal was to highlight what was happening to these workers. He said that he was tired of farm workers being treated "as if they were not important human beings." This speech continues to be one of the most memorable speeches of Chavez's career.

Sowing the Seeds of Change

When he was young, Chavez worked in the fields of California with his family. He saw firsthand how farm workers were treated on the job. His experience in the field compelled him to improve working conditions for all farm workers.

Chavez speaks at a rally for the United Farm Workers.

Hungry for Justice

Chavez often fasted as a way to protest. He ate no food and only drank water. His longest fast lasted for 36 days! He fasted to bring attention to the harmful impact of pesticides on farm workers.

Jobs introduces the iPad tablet in 2010.

Learning Happens Everywhere

Jobs never earned a college degree. Instead, he liked to learn in his own way. Jobs would sit in on college classes and learn about subjects that interested him, such as calligraphy, Shakespeare, and modern dance.

Steve Jobs

If you own an iPhone, you can thank Steve Jobs for that invention. The Apple® co-founder was an **innovative** leader in the technology world. In June 2005, Jobs spoke to the graduating class at Stanford University in California. He **reminisced** about important life lessons he had learned, and he urged the students to follow their dreams.

Jobs spoke about doing what you love: "The only way to do great work is to love what you do. If you haven't found it yet, keep looking."

He spoke about staying authentic: "Don't let the noise of others' opinions drown out your own inner voice."

He advised the students to live each day as though it was their last: "Your time is limited, so don't waste it living someone else's life."

Jobs's last bit of advice: "Stay hungry. Stay foolish." It was sound advice and words he had tried to abide by, too.

Very Sneaky!

If you have a Macintosh® computer, Jobs's speech might be living right under your nose! This is because a text file of his speech is hidden in the software of every Mac computer. No one knows for sure why it's there, but some people think it might be a final tribute to Jobs, who died in 2011.

Pat Summitt

Female athletes have Pat Summitt to thank for many strides made in women's sports. Summitt was a **veritable** force as a player and as a coach.

In 1974, the women's basketball team at the University of Tennessee (UT) needed a head coach. Summitt was hired and coached the team for a remarkable 38-year run. Her teams won 1,098 games, including eight tournament titles, which makes Summitt the most successful coach in all of sports by far.

She was known for her toughness and discipline with her teams. Summit was a big proponent of teamwork. "Put the team before yourself," she often said. She believed that if the team succeeded, individuals succeeded.

Summitt was inducted into five different halls of fame. In 2011, she spoke at the Tennessee Women's Hall of Fame, her fifth and final hall of fame induction. She was humbled and honored as she accepted the award. "I want to keep doing the right things for women all the time."

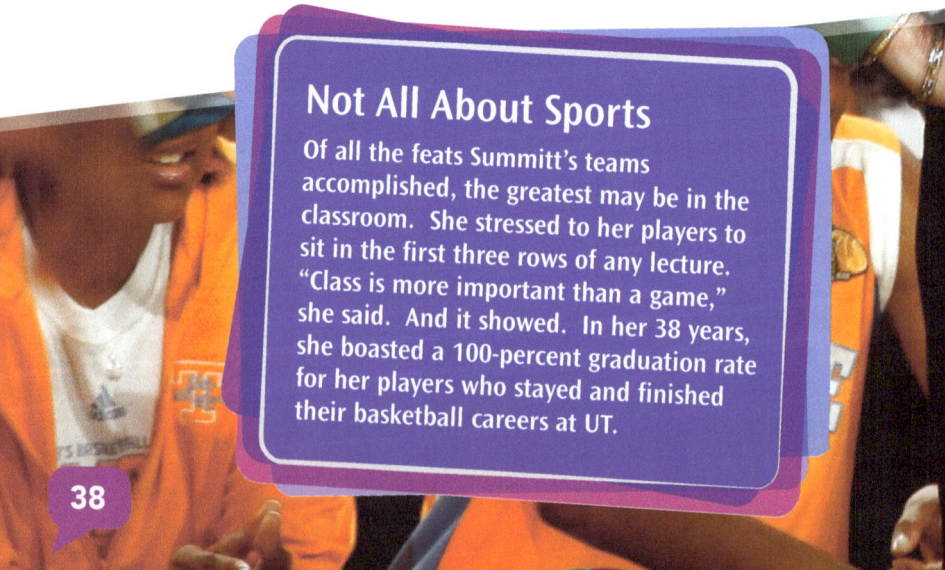

Not All About Sports

Of all the feats Summitt's teams accomplished, the greatest may be in the classroom. She stressed to her players to sit in the first three rows of any lecture. "Class is more important than a game," she said. And it showed. In her 38 years, she boasted a 100-percent graduation rate for her players who stayed and finished their basketball careers at UT.

Another Offer

The UT administration offered Summitt the job to coach the men's team two times. That would have made her the first female head coach of a Division I team. It would have paid her more and given her more fame. But Summitt turned the job down both times. "Why is that considered a step up?" she asked.

The Power of Words

Ralph Waldo Emerson knew the power of words. A poet, a philosopher, and an orator who lived during the 19th century, Emerson is known for writing, "Speech is power. Speech is to persuade, to **convert**, to compel."

This idea was true in the 1800s, and it is also true today. Our words have meaning and value, and they are very powerful things! Words have the power to stir up emotions, influence opinions, and change the course of history.

With a speech, the power comes not just from the words themselves but also from the delivery. Some speeches are shouted from a stage in front of thousands of people. Others are spoken to just a few people in a small setting. Either way, very few things have the impact of a well-crafted speech. It's amazing what words can do!

A Woman for Women

Women's rights have always been important to Hillary Clinton. When she was First Lady, she spoke at a United Nations conference. She voiced an idea that seemed obvious, but it needed to be said out loud. "Human rights are women's right, and women's rights are human rights."

A Man of Many Words

The longest speech delivered to the United Nations was a doozy. It was almost eight hours long! It was given by V.K. Krishna Menon, an Indian politician.

Ralph Waldo Emerson

Glossary

campaign—activity designed to produce a particular result, such as an election

ceremony—a formal event

commemorate—to do something that reminds people of an important past event

communist—a person who believes in a system of government in which goods and wealth are distributed evenly to all the people

compelling—holding one's interest

convert—to change from one point of view to another

empathy—being understanding of a person's experiences and emotions

humanity—the ability to feel for another; kindness

imperial—relating to an empire or emperor

inauguration—an official event at which someone begins an important job

influence—to change or affect someone or something

injustice—unfair treatment

innovative—having ideas to create something new and different

migrant—a person who goes from place to place for work

motivate—to give a reason for doing something

nemesis—an enemy

noble—having traits that people look up to

pact—a formal agreement between two countries to stop fighting

podium—a stand for someone giving a speech

radical—having social or political views that are very different than most people's

reminisced—talked or thought about things that happened in the past

superintendent—a person who manages a place

turbulent—full of confusion and disorder

veritable—true

Index

abolitionist, 32
Apple, 37
Berlin Wall, 10–11
Bloody Sunday, 14
body language, 16
Britain, 18, 20, 29
"Britain Awake," 18
California, 34, 37
Canada, 22
Capitol, 6
Chavez, Cesar, 34–35
China, 13, 38
Clinton, Hillary, 40
Cold War, 9, 18, 20
Collins, Tim, 28–29
Commonwealth Club of California, 34
communist, 18
Douglass, Frederick, 30–33
Edmund Pettus Bridge, 14
Emerson, Ralph Waldo, 40–41
Founding Fathers, 30
Fourth of July, 30, 32
Gettysburg Address, 40
Gorbachev, Mikhail, 10
HeForShe, 22
iPod, 37
Iraq War, 29
Jobs, Steve, 36–37
journalist, 28
Kennedy, John F., 6–9
Lincoln, Abraham, 40
London, 18
MacArthur, Douglas, 24–27
Macintosh, 37
Medal of Honor, 27
Menon, V.K. Krishna, 41
New York, 12, 24, 26, 31
Obama, Barack, 14–15, 19
Oval Office, 29
prime minister, 20, 22
Reagan, Ronald, 10–11, 19
Russians, 20
Selma, Alabama, 14–15
slavery, 30–33
Soviet Union, 9–10, 18, 20

Stanford University, 37
Summitt, Pat, 38–39
Texas, 26
Thatcher, Margaret, 18–21
Trudeau, Justin, 22–23
United Nations, 13, 22, 41
U.S. Military Academy at West Point, 24, 26–27
Voting Rights Act of 1965, 14
Washington, DC, 5–6
Watson, Emma, 22
White House, 6, 15, 29

Check It Out!

Books

Blaisdell, Bob, ed. 2011. *Great Speeches of the 20th Century*. Dover Publications.

Dowis, Richard. 1999. *The Lost Art of the Great Speech: How to Write One—How to Deliver it*. New York: AMACOM.

McIntire, Suzanne, ed. 2001. *The American Heritage Book of Great American Speeches for Young People*. New York: Jossey-Bass.

Nielson, Jennifer. 2015. *A Night Divided*. New York: Scholastic Press.

Williams-Garcia, Rita. 2011. *One Crazy Summer*. New York: Amistad.

Websites

American Rhetoric. www.americanrhetoric.com.

History.com. *Famous Speeches & Audio*. www.history.com/speeches.

TED. *Talks by brilliant kids and teens*. www.ted.com/playlists/129/ted_under_20.

TED. *Talks to watch with kids*. www.ted.com/playlists/86/talks_to_watch_with_kids.

Try It!

The principal of your school asks you to give a speech at the next assembly. Your speech can be about anything you want, but it needs to be at least five minutes long. You have never given a speech before, but you are up for the challenge.

- What will you speak about?

- Will you need to do any research for your speech? If so, what resources will you use? Think about books, websites, online videos, and other sources that will help you learn more about your topic.

- Once you figure out what you will speak about, it's time to prepare. Will you write out the whole speech and memorize it? Or will you jot down important points you want to address?

- Using the body language diagram on pages 16–17, practice your speech in front of your friends or family. Ask your audience for feedback on your speech.

About the Author

Nicole Sipe loves listening to and reading about speeches, but she is not a big fan of giving them. She prefers to communicate in ways that don't involve talking—such as writing this book! Nicole has written books and articles for people of all ages, about everything from dogs to doughnuts, and the Hawaiian Islands to the moon. She lives in central Indiana with her husband and two sons.

www.ingramcontent.com/pod-product-compliance
Lightning Source LLC
Chambersburg PA
CBHW041505010526
44118CB00001B/22